Saviour of the World

Abba Father

MARGARET NEWMELI

DEDICATION

To Mami Helene and Papa Raphael.

I love you always in Christ.

Hallelujah Christ is risen he has triumphed over death and hell even the grave. Jesus who died upon the cross now is alive Hallelujah!

"Because I live, you shall live also." Jn. 14:19.

ACKNOWLEDGMENTS

I thank my family, humanity, and all of creation. I acknowledge Dr. Shawn Smith and the grace of Christ in the Gospel.

"He ascended up on high, he led captivity captive, and gave gifts unto men. For the perfecting of the saints, for the work of the ministry, for the edifying of the body of Christ: Till we all come in the unity of the faith, and of the knowledge of the Son of God, unto a perfect man, unto the measure of the stature of Christ." *Eph. 4:8.12,13.*

My soul magnifies the Lord, my spirit rejoices in God my Saviour.

TABLE OF CONTENTS

PREFACE

"Abba, Father, all things are possible unto thee; take away this cup from me: nevertheless not what I will, but what thou wilt." *Mk 14:36.* "For you have not received the spirit of bondage again to fear; but you have received the Spirit of adoption, by whom we cry, Abba, Father." *Rms. 8:15.* "And because you are sons, God has sent forth the Spirit of his Son into your hearts, crying, *Abba, Father.*" *Gal. 4:6.*

"And she shall bring forth a son, and thou shall call his name JESUS: for he shall save his people from their sins." *Mt. 1:21.* "For unto you is born this day in the city of David a Saviour, which is Christ the Lord." *Lk. 2:11.* "And we know that this is indeed the Christ, *The Saviour of the World.*" *Jn. 4:42.*

INTRODUCTION

On a certain night of April, I had a dream where I sang three songs, which were all heavenly. They seemed to be Easter songs. The last one was particularly striking. It was so beautiful I wanted to know the lyrics and though it was late, I knew the choir was still rehearsing at Cinecam and I couldn't help but go out at that hour of night to get the lyrics. So I left home and took the road of Quartier Malien, but passed through the other road behind. I ran, even like Naruto in one of the anime openings, until I left the quarter and found myself on the big road. I continued like that until Cineccam.

The choir was practicing in the same building they used to do when I was part of it and the building, which was my primary school, was the same as it was ten years ago. I climbed the stairs and passed the classrooms and other groups were holding activities in the other rooms. When I finally got to the classroom where the choir was practicing, one of the choristers was singing the same song I came to get the lyrics.

I stood at the entrance of the door, overwhelmed by the melody. I cried and sank onto the floor, *tellement* it was good. I had never heard such a beautiful song before. It was heaven itself as I listened. I was weighed down and when the girl finished singing, the choirmaster took me to another room and asked me to wait there until the end of the practice; for I told him I wanted the lyrics of that song. We stayed there and when I returned to the choir room, the practice was over and many choristers had left.

I met with some who were still in the classroom. We talked and they asked me about the song I came to get the lyrics. When I tried to sing the song, I couldn't remember. Come on; I knew the song and I was singing it at home before I got there and the chorister also sang it, but now they couldn't help me because I couldn't remember the song. I was perplexed. I thought hard yet nothing came to mind. The song was gone.

That was when I woke up from sleep and then I tried to sing the song without success. I hummed melodies and it still wasn't the song. In the dream I was certain I knew the song. I have received several songs in dreams over the years. Those songs were usually original, not like the ones I compose. They came to me complete and I heard the perfection thereof in the dream. It used to happen that I woke up after hearing the song and so I could hum it, and so I took the phone and recorded what I could remember of it. Before I had a phone, I would sing it endlessly in the night so I don't forget in the morning. The songs I didn't record or sing disappeared in the morning and I couldn't retrieve them.

Yet the songs are never as perfect as I heard them in the dream. In the dream, it is complete; the melody is clear, unwavering. The lyrics are accurately articulated, and sung with angelic voices. But when I wake up, I can only hum the melody, I don't remember the lyrics, maybe a few words and many times, I sing wrong. I only gather bits and pieces of what I heard so they don't completely vanish. So I would put my own lyrics to the melody and sing the songs. They're still good for I enjoy singing them but they're not even close to the beauty I heard in the dream.

There were three songs in this particular dream and they were like Easter songs. It used to happen that after Easter, like Easter Monday or Tuesday, I would receive a song in the dream or a revelation that I would write down. It didn't happen this Easter which was on April 1 yet something occurred in the night of the 20th. They were three songs and they were so beautiful and the last one surpassed the two by far.

I once had a dream where my brothers and I saw a cartoon, which was the consummate of every cartoon I'd ever seen. It was total bliss. The setting was like a bright village; it was something between *Naruto* and *Avatar*. The script wasn't traditional and there was no fighting. And it was so good. I remember we didn't watch it home. It seemed we were spying through a window in a quarter where there was sand all over and it was dry. That's how we watched it.

When I woke up, I tried to remember the script because I sure had a world-shattering idea there if I could write what I saw. In the dream, I knew the story, but I tried to recall it in the waking state yet nothing. All I had was the sensation of having watched something out of this world. I told the dream to my brothers and they marveled.

I have started writing *Other Dimensions*. The stories are more fantasy than *Another Dimension*. I am stuck now and there are chapters I began, which I can't finish. The idea is fantastic; eight different stories with one theme. The Elites of the Supreme Fighter go two by two to the obscure worlds to get the Mex for their master and each pair live a magical moment with the people they encounter in the obscure worlds, which world itself is a mystery. I have finished four of the stories, but I can't get to finish the other four.

I am mesmerized each time I take the chapters and begin reading the story to get the inspiration for the continuation. However, when I get to where I stopped, I can't continue. I'm the first who want to know the continuation and end of the stories, but I'm stuck. I can't get myself to writing it. And sometimes when I read the stories, I feel there are items of what I saw in the dream cartoon in them. Yet it is not it because what I saw was pure delight.

When I woke up on Friday April 20 after the dream, I thought this: The Lord is the song that I sing. I felt my divinity, I felt I was on top of the world, I felt life was beyond what we see and do in the waking state. I felt I was eternal and nothing could hinder me for I am a celestial being. I was so confident and assured I looked down on every circumstance because they were nothing compared to the song I heard in the dream.

The Lord is the song that I sing. A day before or so, I went to the balcony and I didn't want to sing. I always sing every time I go to the balcony. Now there was no new song to sing. I didn't feel like singing the old. There is *Adoration*, which I also got in a dream, my latest song. But I didn't put the lyrics so I couldn't sing it accurately. I love singing but it's always the Lord's song I sing. Other songs don't interest me that I should sing them. Even when I felt like I had strayed from the Lord, I couldn't help singing Him when I get to sing. That was strange to me because I felt I didn't behave as He wanted yet I love singing and I can't sing any song except the Lord.

And so I will find myself worshipping and lifting up hands in singing. It has always been like this since childhood. What is the Lord to me: He is the one that I sing for there is no song I can sing and be transported if not the Lord. So that is what He is to me. Of course, He's much more; He is my father, my saviour, my comforter. He's the Almighty, the Lord, Sovereign over all; He is Christ the All in All, creator of the world, the resurrection and life, and is past-finding. However, if I have to speak about my communion with Him, the place I see Him, I love Him to the fullest, it is when I sing Him.

It's incredible how I haven't released these songs yet. They're so lovely and I believe people are going to be beatified on listening to them, just as they will on reading *Another Dimension*. When I got discouraged sometimes, I used to say to myself maybe those songs were not meant that I should release them or for people to hear. Maybe they were meant for me alone for truly I have sung them and enjoyed them completely and blessed the Lord while singing.

But I know the beauty, I know the bliss that's why I want to share with the world; the stories, which are narrated in *Another Dimension/Other Dimensions* and the songs I sing to the Lord. That's what I want to do in this world; to get people beatified by these songs and stories. I'll seek the song, which I had in my dream of April 20. It was heaven itself and that to me was the evidence. It was the Lord I met in the song. What else could that be?

Lately, the Lord told me He's my greatest fan and He loves listening to me sing Him. Then I thought this Easter, I'm going to write these songs down and publish them in a book. It's going to be a three volume book. I'm not a musician; I don't compose songs. I sing because the Lord has given me these songs. Some songs used to be whole scripture passages, some I tried to compose, some I heard vaguely, some are familiar melodies, and some came to me in dreams. These are only the lyrics. The melodies are with me while some have been uploaded.

The world doesn't know these songs because they're not fashioned after it. These melodies don't follow the pattern of this age for they're not of this world. I have been singing them to the Lord since childhood and lately, He told me He has been enjoying them. He said when I sing to Him, the church, the angels, the spirits, creation, the elements accompany me and as I sing, He is happy.

The Lord is the Saviour of the World; He is the Saviour of all men. I
desire to know Him as father by the Spirit of His Son, the Lord Jesus
Christ, who cries within me: Abba Father.

Saviour of the World

Abba Father

A Hymn Book

1 ABBA FATHER

ABBA FATHER

Now the Spirit of the Lord is in my heart
He's the Spirit of his Son the Lord Jesus
And the Spirit who cries from deep within
Abba Father Abba Father
Now the Spirit of the Lord is in my heart
He's the Spirit of his Son the Lord Jesus
And the Spirit who cries from deep within
Abba Father Abba Father

Chorus
Abba Father Abba Father
We declare you are Our Father
Abba Father Abba Father
We your Church lift your name on high
Abba Father Abba Father
We declare we are your sons
Abba Father Abba Father
By grace through faith in Jesus Christ

By the faith of Christ now we are the sons of God
We are heirs of God and coheirs with Jesus Christ
We have entered his rest we have obtained his inheritance
Abba Father Abba Father
We are seated and we reign with Christ the King
We're the visible image of God on the earth
As he is so are we when he appears so shall we be
Abba Father Abba Father

Chorus
Abba Father Abba Father
We declare you are Our Father
Abba Father Abba Father
We your Church lift your name on high
Abba Father Abba Father

We declare we are your sons
Abba Father Abba Father
By grace through faith in Jesus Christ

Here's the kingdom of our God and of his Christ
All the systems of this world have been subdued
See the Church of God rising in great glory
Abba Father Abba Father
Here's the kingdom of our God and of his Christ
All the systems of this world have been subdued
See the Church of God rising in great glory
Abba Father Abba Father

YESHUA JESUS

Chorus
Yeshua Yeshua Yeshua Yeshua
Yeshua Yeshua Mashiach *(2xs)*

This is the testimony
God has given us eternal life
And this life is in his Son Jesus Christ
For he is the expressed image
Of the unseen God
The brightness of his glory
Upholding all things
By the word of his power
When he has purged our sins
Sat down on the right hand
Of Majesty
Now who can overcome the world
Only the man who believes
That Jesus is Son of God
This is our victory

Chorus
Yeshua Yeshua Yeshua Yeshua
Yeshua Yeshua Mashiach *(2xs)*

God says to the First-Begotten
You are my Son
This day I have begotten you
Let all worship you
Your throne O God is forever
Righteousness scepter of your kingdom
God has anointed you
With the oil of gladness
You Lord in the beginning
Laid the foundations of the earth
Heavens the work of your hands
Your years won't fail
Truly, truly and forever
You are my Beloved Son
On you rest all my favor
Jesus Christ

Chorus
Yeshua Yeshua Yeshua Yeshua
Yeshua Yeshua Mashiach *(2xs)*

This is the love of God
He has given us his only Son
As Saviour of the World Jesus Christ
The Firstborn of creation
And by the blood of his cross
Has reconciled everything
To his Father
For it pleased the Father
That in him should dwell all fullness
That he might have pre-eminence
Over all things
Yes in him through him and for him
Are all things created
The Firstborn from the dead
Jesus Christ

Jesus Jesus Jesus Jesus
Jesus Jesus Jesus Christ *(4xs)*

BLESSED BE THE LORD GOD

Chorus
Blessed be the Lord God of Israel
For he has visited his people
He has caused the dawn of salvation to rise on us
By giving us a Saviour from the house of David
Blessed be the God of our ancestor Abraham
For he has remembered his covenant
The dayspring from high the light of men
Now dwells with us
Jesus our Immanuel

I the Lord your God
Will raise up to you a prophet
From the midst of you of your brethren
A prophet like Moses of old
And to him shall you hearken
For I have anointed him with my Spirit
To give light to Gentiles
And glory to my people Israel

The Spirit of the Sovereign Lord
Is resting upon me
The Lord anointed me to preach the Good News
To all the peoples of the earth
And lo, I come, O Lord my God
With the body that you have prepared for me
To do your will and offer
My life a living sacrifice for you

And it shall come to pass
That in the last days
I will pour my Spirit upon all flesh
And I will save all who call unto me
As I come in the name of the Lord
To fill my people with the love of God
To regenerate the world
And manifest the sons of God on earth

AS RIGHTEOUS AS GOD

You became sin that I might be righteous
You became poor now I am rich
You were forsaken now I am accepted
You became curse now I am blessed
I'll praise your grace Jesus your name
You are the only one who has saved us
Now that you live in me as my life
Lord I manifest what you are in me

Chorus
I am fathered by God
I'm as righteous as God
I'm revealed now as the new new man
In Christ *(2xs)*

You died as me now I am begotten
You bore sickness now I am whole
You took my fears and you became my peace
You set me free now I am free
I'll praise your grace Jesus your name
You are my Father, my Lord, my Comforter
I am your son your body your temple
Lord I manifest what you are in me

Chorus
I am fathered by God
I'm as righteous as God
I'm revealed now as the new new man
In Christ *(2xs)*

Now creation sees the rising of the glorious church
All the nations bow and confess that Jesus Christ is Lord
I'll praise your grace Jesus your name
You are all that I wanted all that I wanted
You are my righteousness
I'll praise your grace Jesus your name
I am all that you wanted all that you wanted

Son of God now manifest

Chorus
Je suis engendré par Dieu
Aussi juste que Dieu
Révélé comme le nouvel homme en Christ *(2xs)*

Chorus
I am fathered by God
I'm as righteous as God
I'm revealed now as the new new man
In Christ *(2xs)*

ETERNAL LIFE

Know man you're in this world
To be in Jesus who is eternal life
This is the reason for your life
All the others are accessories
Jesus Christ is the Son of God
Who was made man and died for your sins
He rose from death reconciled you to God
Your creator and redeemer

Chorus
God is calling a better life for you and me
A better life for you and me
God has become eternal life to you and me
In Jesus Christ to you and me

In Jesus Christ sins are forgiven
We are set free we're healed by his stripes
We are blessed we are born again
A new creation in Christ
Our destiny is to be in God
And be clothed with His glory
We are heirs so cry Abba Father
His righteousness in Christ

Chorus
God is calling a better life for you and me
A better life for you and me
God has become eternal life to you and me
In Jesus Christ to you and me
God is calling a better life for you and me
A better life for you and me
God has become eternal life to you and me
Eternal life to you and me

Bridge
We believe in Him
We confess Jesus Christ is Lord
By grace through faith in Christ alone
And we are saved here and now
We believe in Him
Whom God has raised from the dead
We bow down and worship him
He is Lord Saviour of the world

Chorus in Tongues
Nao sere Nao sero Nao kerobage
Manemawa Mane sema
Nao Kristus Nao sero Nao kerobage
Manemawa mane sema *(2xs)*

Bridge
We believe in Him
We confess Jesus Christ is Lord
By grace through faith in Christ alone
And we are saved here and now
We believe in Him
Whom God has raised from the dead
We bow down and worship him

He is Lord Saviour of the world *(4xs)*

Chorus
God is calling a better life for you and me

A better life for you and me
God has become eternal life to you and me
In Jesus Christ to you and me
God is calling a better life for you and me
A better life for you and me
God has become eternal life to you and me
Eternal life to you and me

UNTO YOU

I am proud I boast
In Jesus Christ my Lord and King
Lamb of God Lord over all
Unto you be the greatest glory

I am proud I boast
In Jesus Christ my Lord and King

Lamb of God Lord over all
Unto you be the greatest glory *(6xs)*

I am proud I boast
In Jesus Christ my Lord and King

SAVED BY YOUR LIFE

O, O Lord as I lift my eyes to heaven
Singing O, O Lord
Wondering what you've done for Earthlings
How you sent your Son to save us
How he became one of us
How you made him what we were
And now we are in Him
O, O Lord in your grace you have reversed
All that was against and was contrary to man
By our union with the one
That you stablished as our Saviour

And today you and the people
Have got one origin

Chorus
I will lift my voice to heaven
Shouting out with all my heart
Giving thanks to your amazing
Grace that rescued O my soul
Singing always, always, always we are saved
Oh, what a glory
That the fullness of the Son
Has come to every man
By our union with Christ
As we partake of his life
And we're whole, whole, whole
Through the life of Christ our Saviour
We are whole, whole, whole
By the mercies of our Father
We are whole, whole, whole
In our oneness with the Spirit
Whole, whole, whole
Forever we are saved by your life

Holy is the Lord
Father Son and Holy Spirit
Holy is the Lord
Christ the Firstborn of creation
Christ the author of salvation
Christ the Mediator, the God Man
Christ the Lover of Humanity
God's Righteousness for all
Nothing can condemn
The man whom Christ has justified
What can stand against
It is God himself that testifies
That he birthed all men in Jesus
That we are his own beloved
There is nothing missing nothing loss
We all are found in Christ

Lift my praise among the peoples
Giving glory to your name
For your love's beyond imagining
And your grace beyond all thoughts
I sing holy, holy, holy is the Lord
Oh, what a glory
That the fullness of the Son
Has come to every man
By our union with Christ
As we partake of his life
And we're whole, whole, whole
Through the life of Christ our Saviour
We are whole, whole, whole
By the mercies of our Father
We are whole, whole, whole
In our oneness with the Spirit
Whole, whole, whole
Forever we are saved by your life

Shout your joy across the earth
Nature lands angels and beings
Join us now as we sing him
We are whole, whole, whole
Oh, what a glory
For one has become all men
And we live inside of him
Saved and safe forever and ever

We are whole, whole, whole
Through the life of Christ our Saviour
We are whole, whole, whole
By the mercies of our Father
We are whole, whole, whole
In our oneness with the Spirit
Whole, whole, whole
Forever we are saved by your life

2 JESUS CHRIST IS LORD

SONG OF THE SON

I see the Lord in his glory
And the train of his robe fills the temple
Behold my eyes have seen his goodness
Who has saved us for eternity
I see the Lord high and lifted up
And the angels all round His Majesty
Behold the sons of God are on the throne
With the Firstborn we cry Abba

Chorus
Abba Abba Father
In the Spirit we cry Abba
Abba Abba Father
With the Firstborn we cry Abba
Abba Abba Father
Abba Abba Father
Abba Abba Father
With the Firstborn we cry Abba

(Repeat verse and chorus)

JESUS IS LORD

See the Son of Man come with power and great glory
See the Son of God return and his brightness fills the earth
His sign appears on high His church is ready for him
And Jesus comes to be glorified in all the saints
Father O Lord you have saved me
Not by any works of my own you have saved me
By your love by your faith Lord I am your son
By the grace that's in Jesus all things are mine

Chorus
I believe in the Lord I believe in Jesus
I believe in the Lord I believe in Jesus

Hear the trumpet resound this is the signal
See the mighty angels come down in the splendour of the Lord
On the day when these things happen I lift up my head
And I see the Son of God revealed in the clouds
Father O Lord you have saved us
By the good pleasure of your will you have saved us
Through the finished work of Jesus we are in Christ
By the power of your Spirit Christ is in us

We will praise you forever
Forever God you've saved us
Receive now your desire
Your glorious Church the bride of Christ

Chorus
I believe in the Lord I believe in Jesus
I believe in the Lord I believe in Jesus

Bridge
See Jesus come lift up your heads
Hear the trumpet sound heaven on earth
See Jesus come lift up your heads
Hear the trumpet sound heaven on earth *(3xs)*

Jesus Lord the whole earth cries
You are Lord forever you reign
You are lovely you are lovely
You are lovely you are lovely
Come, Lord Jesus come
You are faithful you are faithful
You are faithful you are faithful
Come, Lord Jesus come
You are glorious, glorious
You are glorious, glorious
Come, Lord Jesus come

I believe I believe I believe
I believe I believe I believe in you
I believe in Jesus

Chorus
I believe in the Lord I believe in Jesus
I believe in the Lord I believe in Jesus *(4xs)*

BLESS THE LORD

Chorus
Bless the Lord O my soul
Bless the Lord all that's within me
Bless the Lord who forgives all your sins
Bless the Lord who heals all your disease
Bless the Lord O my soul bless the Lord
Bless the Lord all the angels of the Lord
Bless the Lord all the hosts of the Lord
Bless the Lord all creation
Bless the Lord O my soul

The Lord is righteous
He is the defender of the oppressed
He made known his ways to Moses
His acts to the children of Israel
The Lord is merciful
Gracious is he and slow to anger
He is plenteous in steadfast love

As the heavens are high above the earth
So great is his mercy to them that fear him
As far as the east's from west
So far has he removed our transgressions
Yes the mercy of the Lord
Is from everlasting to everlasting
His righteousness to all generations

Upon those who fear him

To those who keep his covenant
To children's children yes to them
Who remember to do his commandments

The Lord has established his throne
In the heavens his kingdom rules over all
Bless him his hosts, his ministers
His works in all places of his dominion

Bless his holy name
Bless the Lord O my soul
And forget not all his benefits
Bless him who satisfies you with good

Chorus
Bless the Lord O my soul
Bless the Lord all that's within me
Bless the Lord who forgives all your sins
Bless the Lord who heals all your disease
Bless the Lord O my soul bless the Lord
Bless the Lord all the angels of the Lord
Bless the Lord all the hosts of the Lord
Bless the Lord all creation
Bless the Lord O my soul

EXALTED

1 2 3 4 5 6 7 now Go
This is the gospel that has been from dawn
No other reason we have seen is of worth
The Everlasting Father's love for his Son
Is the one and only purpose of the world and for us
This is what was before the creation of things
And now has come to be manifested in time
Jesus Christ, the Son of God the Saviour
Of the world appeared with this grace
Now we're the sons of God in Christ

Bridge
Oh oh oh oh oh oh
Oh oh oh oh oh oh
Oh oh oh oh oh oh
Oh oh oh oh.......... *(2xs)*

Chorus
I ascended on high
Now I'm lifted with might
I am reigning in life
I'm exalted with Christ *(2xs)*

Go. After he has done everything that was right
He spread his wings lifted himself above on high
The good news is that I also ascended with him
And everything he is he has made me also to be
Now that he fills the entire universe
He has distributed all good gifts to men
For every man, where, every time is in Christ Jesus
He's the man by whom we're identified

Bridge
Oh oh oh oh oh oh
Oh oh oh oh oh oh
Oh oh oh oh oh oh
Oh oh oh oh.......... *(2xs)*

Chorus
I ascended on high
Now I'm lifted with might
I am reigning in life
I'm exalted with Christ *(2xs)*

Speaking in tongues Instruments

1 2 3 4 5 6 7 now Go

Bridge
Oh oh oh oh oh oh

Oh oh oh oh oh oh
Oh oh oh oh oh oh
Oh oh oh oh.......... *(2xs)*

Chorus
I ascended on high
Now I'm lifted with might
I am reigning in life
I'm exalted with Christ *(2xs)*

MIGHTY GOD

Mighty mighty mighty is the Lord
Mighty mighty mighty is the Lord
Wonderful Counsellor
Mighty mighty mighty is the Lord
He is Wonderful Counsellor

Holy holy holy is the Lord
Holy holy holy is the Lord
Prince of Peace Christ in us
Holy holy holy is the Lord
He is Prince of Peace Immanuel

Mighty mighty mighty is the Lord
Mighty mighty mighty is the Lord
Everlasting Abba Father
Mighty mighty mighty is the Lord
He's the Everlasting Father

TON AMOUR SEIGNEUR

Ton amour Seigneur
Ton amour Seigneur
Ton amour Seigneur nous a justifiés
Ton amour nous appelle *(2xs)*

Nous sommes vivants Seigneur
Nous sommes vivants Seigneur
Nous sommes vivants Seigneur en ton Fils Jésus
Ton amour nous appelle *(2xs)*

Christ en nous Seigneur
Christ en nous Seigneur
Christ en nous Seigneur est l'espoir de gloire
Ton amour nous appelle *(2xs)*

SONS OF GOD/DESTINY

Vapour in the sky chilling in the rain
Waves upon the sea the darkness of the night
Snow that blocked the way mountains that obstruct
Living in the storm these are in the past

Suffering is out all the tears are gone
That was yesterday of Adam and his ways
Today I am in Christ I decree and it's done
Living in the power of Jesus Christ the Lord

I'm riding on the winds I'm flying with the birds
I walk upon the sea there's nothing to stop me
I summon things to being and everything obeys
Demonstrate with power that I reign with him

What is the reason that you loved me so much
What is the reason that you lavished this grace on me
Now I am crowned with glory now I am seated with you
What is the reason that you died for me

Chorus
To be your sons this is all you wanted
To be in Christ this is the reason for man
We have overcome victory is ours
We are sons of God in Christ

Heaven in my heart I am my Father's heir
No one can deny creation testifies
Nothing can reverse your nature that's in me
Living now the life of God on the earth

Jesus take pleasure of what you have done
Before the world began you chose me to be yours
I'm your masterpiece exactly as you are
Living now your life manifest as you

What is the reason that you loved me so much
What is the reason that you lavished this grace on me
Now I am crowned with glory now I am seated with you
What is the reason that you died for me

Chorus
To be your sons this is all you wanted
To be in Christ this is the reason for man
We have overcome victory is ours
We are sons of God we are sons of God
We are sons of God in Christ

Bridge
Victory is mine sin has got no say
Who will accuse us the devil is destroyed
Death has lost its sting the grave its victory
We have overcome by the blood of the Lamb

Victory is ours sin has got no say
Who will accuse us the accuser is destroyed
Death has lost its sting the grave its victory

We have overcome *(11xs)*

Chorus
To be your sons this is all you wanted
To be in Christ this is the reason for man
We have overcome victory is ours
We are sons of God in Christ

3 ONE SPIRIT

THE PRINCE OF PEACE OR ITACHI'S SONG

They shall beat their swords into ploughshares
And their spears into pruning hooks
Nation shall not lift up sword against nation
Neither shall they learn war anymore

Peace I leave with you my peace I give you
Not as the world gives give I unto you
As the Father sent me so I send you
My peace above understanding is with you

Chorus
And behold a virgin shall conceive
And shall bring forth a son
He shall be called Wonderful Counsellor
Mighty God Everlasting Father

Peace I leave with you my peace I give you
Not as the world gives give I unto you
As the Father sent me so I send you
My peace above understanding is with you

Chorus
And behold a virgin shall conceive
And shall bring forth a son
He shall be called Wonderful Counsellor
Mighty God Everlasting Father

The Prince of Peace Hallelujah
The Prince of Peace Hosanna
The Prince of Peace Charis Shalom Lai lai lai
He shall be called the Prince of Peace

The Prince of Peace Hallelujah
The Prince of Peace Hosanna

Le Prince de Paix Pace Salaam Lai lai lai
He shall be called the Prince of Peace
He shall be called the Prince of Peace
He shall be called....

Chorus
And behold the Virgin did conceive
And she brought forth the Son of God
Who is called Wonderful Counsellor

Mighty God Everlasting Father
Mighty God Everlasting Father
Mighty God Everlasting Father
Mighty God Everlasting Father

Oh oh oh oh oh Everlasting Father
Oh oh oh oh oh Everlasting Father
Everlasting Father Everlasting Father
Everlasting Father Everlasting Father
Ha ha ha ha ha Everlasting Father
Ha ha ha ha ha Everlasting Father

Everlasting, Everlasting Father
Everlasting, Everlasting Father
Everlasting Father Everlasting Father
Everlasting Father Everlasting Father
Oh oh oh oh Everlasting Father
Oh oh oh oh Everlasting Father

SENSEI

Jesus-kun Jesus-san
Jesus everything I need
Jesus Lord Prince of Peace
Jesus everything I know
Jesus the Master beloved brother
Jesus glory
Christ in me I live in you

You are all that I need

Chorus
Taichou Sensei Shishou Sama
Nii-san Senpai Jesus Jesus

Jésus roi Jésus Dieu
Jésus tout ce que je veux
Jésus joie Prince de Paix
Jésus tout ce que je sais
Jésus le Maitre bien-aimé frère
Jésus gloire
Christ en moi je vis en toi
Tu es tout ce que je veux

Chorus
Taichou Sensei Shishou Sama
Nii-san Senpai Jésus Jésus

Instruments (8xs)

Chorus
Taichou Sensei Shishou Sama
Nii-san Senpai Jésus Jésus
Taichou Sensei Shishou Sama
Nii-san Senpai Jesus Jesus

Jesus Jesus Jesus Jesus
Jesus Jesus Jesus Jesus

Jésus Jésus Jésus Jésus
Jésus Jésus Jésus Jésus

Yeshua Yeshua Yeshua Yeshua
Yeshua Yeshua Yeshua Yeshua

ISAIAH 53

He shall see the travail of his soul
And shall be satisfied
By his knowledge shall my righteous servant
Justify many

Who has believed our report
And to whom is the arm of the Lord revealed
He shall grow up before him as a tender plant
And as a root out of a dry ground
He has no form or comeliness
Has no beauty that we should desire him
He is despised rejected of men
A man of sorrows and acquainted with grief

And we hid as it were our faces from him
He was despised and we did not respect him
Surely he has borne our griefs and sorrows
He was wounded for our transgressions
Upon him the punishment of our sins
And by his wounds we all are healed

Chorus
He shall see the travail of his soul
And shall be satisfied
By his knowledge shall my righteous servant
Justify many *(2xs)*

We all like sheep gone astray
We have turned everyone to his own way
Our iniquity was laid on him
He was oppressed and taken away
Who shall declare his generation
He was cut off the land of the living
For the sin of my people he suffered
He made his grave with the wicked

With the rich in his death 'cause he'd done no violence

Had no deceit but it pleased the Lord to bruise him
When you shall make his soul an offering
For sin he shall see his disciples
He shall prolong his days and the pleasure
Of the Lord shall prosper in his hand

Chorus
He shall see the travail of his soul
And shall be satisfied
By his knowledge shall my righteous servant
Justify many *(2xs)*

And he bore the sin of many
And made intercession for the transgressors *(4xs)*

Chorus
He shall see the travail of his soul
And shall be satisfied
By his knowledge shall my righteous servant
Justify many *(4xs)*

And he bore the sin of many
And made intercession for the transgressors *(4xs)*

SO GREAT SALVATION

Christ appeared in the body
Made just by the Spirit
Was seen by the angels Amen
He was preached among the nations
Believed in the whole world
Was taken up in glory Amen *(2xs)*

Chorus
This is a saying this is a saying
That deserves full acceptance
This is the mystery this is the mystery
Of our salvation that is great

Christ appeared in the body
Made just by the Spirit
Was seen by the angels Amen
He was preached among the nations
Believed in the whole world
Was taken up in glory Amen

Chorus
This is a saying this is a saying
That deserves full acceptance
This is the mystery this is the mystery
Of our salvation that is great *(2xs)*

Of our salvation that is great *(3xs)*

A SAVIOUR FOR US

The angel came to the Virgin
And said Hail Mary
Thou art highly favoured
The Lord is with thee
Thou shall bring forth a son
And shall call his name Jesus
He shall save his people
His kingdom has no end
And Mary said to the angel
Behold the Lord's handmaid
Be it unto me
According to your word
And so the angel left her
And she conceived in her womb
By the power of the Spirit
A Saviour for us

Chorus
And you are the Lamb of God
The Redeemer of the human race
You are the Saviour of the World

Jesus Son of God

And Mary came to Elizabeth
As she heard her salutation
The baby leaped for joy
And she was filled with the Spirit
Blessed art thou among women
And blessed is the fruit of thy womb
For what the Lord has spoken
Shall surely come to pass
And Mary lifted her voice
And magnified the Lord
My soul rejoices
In God who is my Saviour
For he that is mighty
Has done great things for me
Holy is his name
His mercy never ends

Chorus
And you are the Lamb of God
The Redeemer of the human race
You are the Saviour of the World
Jesus Son of God

And Mary brought forth her firstborn
And wrapped him in swaddling clothes
And laid him in a manger
The Word of God made flesh
And the angel brought the tidings
To shepherds in the fields
Today is born to you
A Saviour Christ the Lord
And we beheld his glory
Only begotten of the Father
And of his fullness
We've received grace for grace
For the law was given by Moses
But grace and truth have come

By Jesus Christ the God-Man
The Saviour of the World

Chorus
And you are the Lamb of God
The Redeemer of the human race
You are the Saviour of the World
Jesus Son of God

And you are the light of men
Our Shepherd one and only true
You are the Saviour of the World
Jesus Son of God

And you are the Messiah
God is with us you are Immanuel
You are the Saviour of the World
Jesus Son of God

And you are the Great I Am
The Son of God you are the Son of Man
You are the Saviour of the World
Jesus Son of God

SHEMA ISRAEL

Shema Israel Shema Israel
Shema Israel Adonai Echad

Adonai Echad Adonai Echad
Adonai Adonai Adonai Echad

WORTHY OF ADMIRATION

Among the children of men
None is like to you
Among the children of God

You take the first place
You have been crowned
With honour beauty and majesty
And the eyes of all are set on you in awe

Look at your might God
And receive all the glory and the worth
Look at your throne
And receive all the powers
Because you humbled yourself
And came down to earth
And bore the shame and the sorrows
Of your people

So our voice
Will rise to magnify your holy name
And our lips
Will talk of all your exploits
And in our hearts
We will come to you burning with desire
For at your sight
We are seized with admiration

Chorus
You are worthy of all admiration
You are worthy of all admiration
Because you gave your life to save your people
So God raised you high above your fellows
And you are risen Blessed Saviour
You are glorious our Deliverer
And you are worthy yes you are worthy
And you are worthy of all admiration

You are the wonder of the world
None compares to you
You are the shout of the angels
The song of the saints
You have been given all riches
Dominion and all wealth

And you are exalted above all creation

Look at your works God
And be satisfied with the labour of your hands
Look at your cross
And be pleased with all that you have done
You took the nature of man
And became one with us
And then you raised us
And made us sons of your Father

(Pause)

And our hands
Will be lifted up to worship you alone
And our feet
Will run to proclaim your kingdom
And in our hearts
We will come to you burning with desire
For at your sight
We are seized with admiration

Chorus
You are worthy of all admiration
You are worthy of all admiration
Because you gave your life to save your people
So God raised you high above your fellows
And you are risen Blessed Saviour
You are glorious our Deliverer
And you are worthy yes you are worthy
And you are worthy of all admiration

4 GOD IS LOVE

YOUR LOVE

Chorus
Father, Father
All the earth shouts your praise
Abba Holy One
Lifted above the earth I bow to you

You reign on high you reign on high
Your love has brought us forth
You reign on high you reign on high
Your love has overcome
You reign on high you reign on high
Your love has fathered us
You reign on high you reign on high
Your love made us your sons

(Repeat chorus and verse)

HOMAGE TO JESUS

Jesus Son of the Father
We love you and this is our heart
Jesus you are so beautiful
You love us by giving your life
Jesus be glorified
Be exalted in every heart
Jesus you are so great
You are all that mankind longs for

Jesus all that I'm looking for
You're the greatest treasure of my heart
Jesus you are so wonderful
By your love you have saved the world
Jesus all adoration

All glory all honour and praise
All grace all worship
Of the earth belongs to you

Heh heh heh heh
heh heh heh heh *(4xs)*

Jesus all adoration
All glory all honour and praise
All grace all worship
Of the earth belongs to you

I SHALL YET PRAISE HIM

Chorus
Why are you cast down O my soul
Why are you disquieted within me
Hope you in God
For I shall yet praise him
Who is the health of my countenance
And my God

O my God my soul is cast down within me
Therefore will I remember you
From the land of Jordan and from the Hermonites
From the hill Mizar
My tears have been my food day and night
Your waves and billows over me
Why have you forgotten me why do I go mourning
While they say where is your God

Chorus
Why are you cast down O my soul
Why are you disquieted within me
Hope you in God
For I shall yet praise him
Who is the health of my countenance
And my God

As the dear pants after the water brooks
So pants my soul for thee O Lord
My soul is thirty for God for the Lord my living God
When shall I come before you
Yet the Lord will command his love in the day
At night his song shall be with me
And my prayer to the Lord I will enter his house
With the voice of praise

PERFECTION

Our faces shining bright
Our heads are lifted high
This is the earth
This is the land of every man
We no more wanna fight
For we have seen the light
Join us from east to west
You are me I am you

Our story just began
The convergence of ages
The past the present the future
Culminate in one today

Chorus
Forever people shall not be denied
We are now living our destiny
This is the place where dreams are realized
Now is the perfection of everything

The purpose of our lives
Has come to our sight
This is the day of our freedom
Kingdom come
All men are reconciled
In the body of Christ
There is no division no separation

I will dance with you in the moonlight
Sleeping in your arms when I say goodnight
As the day breaks and I open my eyes
It is you I see and my heart is right

Chorus
Forever people shall not be denied
We are now living our destiny
This is the place where dreams are realized
Now is the perfection of everything

Oh oh oh oh oh oh oh oh
Oh oh oh oh oh oh oh oh

We are sons of the resurrection
Generation of regeneration
See the child in us fulfilled
Every man is now complete
Goodness covers the earth
And the world is rejoicing

Oh oh oh oh oh oh oh oh
Oh oh oh oh oh oh oh oh

We are sons of the resurrection
Generation of regeneration
See the child in us fulfilled
Every man is now complete
Goodness covers the earth
And the world is rejoicing

Oh oh oh oh oh oh oh oh
Oh oh oh oh oh oh oh oh

BORN TO BE SON OF GOD

What does it profit a man
To gain the whole world

And suffer the loss of his own soul
He can have the best things
This world could offer
Yet deep down inside
He longs for something more
There's a life beyond what we can think
There's a journey all of us are in
For we don't where we come
And we don't where we go
Yet in this world of earth I've found
A hope that I believe is true
That Jesus is the way home

Chorus
O Lord into this world I was born
Into this world I was born to be yours
I am born son of God O Lord
Into this world I was born
Into this world I was born
Into this world I was born to be yours
I am born son of God O Lord

What is the meaning of life
The reason why we live
The purpose of our labour on earth
Many have gone their way
You don't give up the fight
Although many times
You find so much pain and sorrow
I have pondered all this in my heart
I have asked for reasons why I lived
And I wondered for so long
Pouring tears over my soul
Yet I believe what I received
That one of us rose from the dead
That Jesus is our only life

Chorus
O Lord into this world I was born

Into this world I was born to be yours
I am born son of God O Lord
Into this world I was born
Into this world I was born
Into this world I was born to be yours
I am born son of God O Lord

Bridge
God has become eternal life to you and me
And earth takes meaning only in His love

I am born son of God
I am born son of God
I am born son of God O Lord *(2xs)*

I am yours I am yours
I am yours I am yours O Lord

I am one with the Lord
And I reign with Jesus
I am born son of God O Lord
I am seated in Christ
As righteous as God
I am born son O Lord

I am yours I am yours
I am yours I am yours O Lord

Begotten of Abba
Hidden with Christ in You
I am born son of God O Lord
You are my prize forever
The luck of my life
I am born son of God O Lord

Chorus
Into this world I was born
Into this world I was born
Into this world to be yours

I am born Son of God O Lord *(2xs)*

JESUS JESUS

Chorus
Jesus Jesus Jesus Jesus
Jesus Jesus Jesus Jesus
Jesus Jesus mighty Jesus
Lovely Jesus Jesus
Holy Jesus gentle Jesus
Beautiful Jesus Jesus

Beloved of the Father love of God
Abode of the Spirit Jesus
Worship of the angels praise of the saints
Joy of heaven Jesus
Splendour of the world beauty of the earth
Colour of creation Jesus
Light in the dark radiance of hearts
Longing of my soul Jesus

Chorus
Jesus Jesus mighty Jesus
Lovely Jesus Jesus
Holy Jesus gentle Jesus
Beautiful Jesus Jesus

Lover of mankind Saviour of the World
Song that I sing Jesus
Healer of souls calm in the storm
Delight of the children Jesus
Wonder precious satisfaction
Compassion gracious Jesus
Heaven and earth adoration
Bliss of creation Jesus

Chorus
Jesus Jesus mighty Jesus

Lovely Jesus Jesus
Holy Jesus gentle Jesus
Beautiful Jesus Jesus

Dance in the night cool of the day
Rays of the sun Jesus
Snow on mountain tops sublime sunset
Refreshing in the winds Jesus
Song of the birds roar of the ocean
Treasure of the people Jesus
True happiness life of mankind
Beloved of the Father Jesus

YOU ARE MY DREAM

Lord I call you Lord
You are God you are the same
And you reign
In heaven and earth in every heart
Your love your love
Is great you are the way
On the cross you gave yourself
And you saved
The human race creation praise
Your grace your grace

Chorus
I call my future my dreams
And my destiny in you
You are my everything *(2xs)*

Abba you are my Father
And you placed me in Christ
Now I am
All that you are I am your son
Your son your son
It's your life that moves me
And you are pleased with me

For you see
Your Son in me Christ is in me
Jesus in me

Chorus
I call my future my dreams
And my destiny in you
You are my everything *(2xs)*

Bridge
I adore you I worship you
You are everything yeah
I bow down I glorify
I lift your name Jesus Jesus

You are my dream Lord you are my dream
All my desire is to be found in you
You are everything you are everything

Pause speaking in tongues

You are the treasure of every heart
Nothing can ever compare to you
You are everything you are everything
Yes Lord you are everything to me yeah

Chorus
I call my future my dreams
And my destiny in you
You are my everything *(2xs)*

5 I LOVE THE LORD

WE BELIEVE IN YOU

Father Lord of the heavens
Our eyes are lifted to you
Father you looked for us
You came and saved your own
We acknowledge that
Your love for us is great
And we recognize that
You became our life
And today we won't fear
For you have shown us your heart
So we put our trust in you
For you O Lord are true

Chorus
We believe in you O Lord
That your love for us is great
We believe you sent your Son
To be our Saviour

Father Lord of the earth
Your children call unto you
Father you are faithful
In Christ all men shall live
You have abolished sin
Heard the cry of the poor
You have healed the sick
Set the prisoner free
And today we rejoice
For you have made us your sons
We will put our trust in you
For you O Lord are true

Chorus
We believe in you O Lord

That your love for us is great
We believe you sent your Son
To be our Saviour *(2xs)*

BABY JESUS

All the earth come and see
He who laid your foundations
Baby Jesus in a manger
Lying on his mother's breasts
He who formed the ancient mountains
And commanded the dry land
He who wields these many waters
And whose voice compels the winds

All creation come and see
He who made you and sustains
Baby Jesus in a manger
And wrapped in swaddling clothes
He who holds the world by his word
And sets all things in their place
He who rules over all powers
And in whom all fullness dwells

All the angels come and see
He who dwells in dazzling light
Baby Jesus in a manger
Resting in the Virgin's arms
He who sits above the cherubs
And to whom the seraphs cry
Whom the hosts of heaven worship
And the living creatures bow

All the peoples come and see
He who brought you into being
Baby Jesus in a manger
With Mary and Joseph by
He who loved you through all ages

And chose you in Christ
Even before the world began
He has saved you by his grace

Resume verses

Chorus
The angels bow we worship you
The angels bow we worship you

SING TO THE LORD A NEW SONG

Chorus
Sing to the Lord a new song
Sing to the Lord all the earth
Sing to the Lord bless his name
Say to the nations that he reigns
Give to the Lord all you peoples
Give to the Lord glory and strength
Give to the Lord glory due his name
Worship him in holiness

Say among the heathen that the Lord reigns
He established the world that it shall not be moved
He shall judge the peoples in righteousness
Let the heavens rejoice let the earth be glad
Let the sea roar before the Lord

Declare his glory and wonders among peoples of nations
For the Lord is great and is greatly to be praised
Honour beauty majesty are in his sanctuary
Let the fields be joyful and all that is therein
Let the trees exult before the Lord

Chorus
Sing to the Lord a new song
Sing to the Lord all the earth
Sing to the Lord bless his name

Say to the nations that he reigns
Give to the Lord all you peoples
Give to the Lord glory and strength
Give to the Lord glory due his name
Worship him in holiness

O sing to the Lord a new song make known all his wonders
He has thought of his mercy to the house of Israel
All the ends of the earth have seen his salvation
Let the floods clap their hands all creation of the world
Let the hills shout loud before the Lord

DESTINY DOES EXIST

Ohoo ohoo ohoo ohoo
Ohoo ohoo ohoo oh oh oh

It is true destiny does exist
You're the one I've been waiting for
My whole whole life
It is true I can see it in your eyes
You're the one for me
You make me complete

It is true destiny does exist
You're the one my heart's been
Yearning for always
It is true I can see it in your eyes
You love me you yes love me
I love you

Ohoo ohoo ohoo ohoo
Ohoo ohoo ohoo oh oh oh

It is true destiny does exist
You're the one I've been waiting for
My whole whole life
It is true I can see it in your eyes

You're the one for me
You make me complete

It is true destiny does exist
You're the one my heart's been
Yearning for always
It is true I can see it in your eyes
You love me yes you love me

I love you I love you
I love you I love you
I love you I love you
I love you I love you *(4xs)*

FAITHFUL GOD

I know whom I have trusted
I know my God is able
To confirm all that I commit unto him
Against that day
God has anointed me with the oil of gladness
Your hand is upon me I belong to you
My life is poured out as an offering
And I groan to be clothed

Chorus
Faithful you are faithful
O Lord my God I put my trust in you
Faithful you are faithful
I believe O Lord you have called me
Faithful you are faithful
Establish that I commit unto you
Faithful you are faithful
On the day of Christ you have saved us

My face is set as splint my strength is consumed
My body fails me while my life is spent
Yet I know that I will never be ashamed

For my cause is before the Lord
The Lord stands with me the Lord gives me power
The Lord rescues me from all temptations
He preserves my soul my body and my spirit
Safely to his heavenly kingdom

Chorus
Faithful you are faithful
O Lord my God I put my trust in you
Faithful you are faithful
I believe O Lord you have called me
Faithful you are faithful
Establish that I commit unto you
Faithful you are faithful
On the day of Christ you have saved us

You establish me till the end
You make me blameless in the day of Christ
God is faithful who has called us
And he also will do

To the righteous judge to the only one omnipotent
To the Lord Almighty to the one immortal God
Be the kingdom the power and the glory
Forever Hallelujah *(3xs)*

Chorus
Faithful you are faithful
O Lord my God I put my trust in you
Faithful you are faithful
I believe O Lord you have called me
Faithful you are faithful
Establish that I commit unto you
Faithful you are faithful
This is the day of Christ
You have saved us

HE FIRST LOVED ME

I love the Lord because he first loved me
I love the Lord because he first loved me
I love the Lord I love the Lord I love the Lord I love the Lord
I love the Lord I love the Lord
Because he first loved me

I love the Lord because he first loved me
I love the Lord because he first loved me

I love the Lord I love the Lord I love the Lord I love Jesus
I love the Lord I love the Lord
Because he first loved me *(2xs)*

I love the Lord because he first loved me

A LOVE SONG

You are the alpha you are omega
You are the centre you're everlasting
You are everyone you are everywhere
You are every time you are eternal
You are God in us you fill everything
You are the meaning you are the reason
You are the treasure you're the desire
You are the answer you're all in all

I lift up my hands worship you my Lord
I am one with you, you have set me free
I shout out for joy Jesus thank you Lord
You are all I am you're my only life

Chorus
Day after day I keep loving you
I think about you can't get you out of my head
Night after night lift my praise to you
Your love is so good you're my dream come true *(2xs)*

You've drawn me closer even to your heart
By your very blood this is our peace
Your Spirit in me is the guarantee
That all things are mine that I am yours

I lift up my voice I cry Abba Father
You are Christ in me grace has supplied all
I bow down to you worship at your feet
You are so worthy of all the glory

Chorus
Day after day I keep loving you
I think about you can't get you out of my head
Night after night lift my praise to you
Your love is so good you're my dream come true *(2xs)*

Bridge
Oh oh oh oh oh oh oh oh oh
Oh oh oh oh oh oh oh oh oh *(2xs)*

I lift up my voice I cry Abba Father
You are Christ in me grace has supplied all
I bow down to you worship at your feet
You are so worthy

Of all the glory *(4xs)*

Chorus
Day after day I keep loving you
I think about you can't get you out of my head
Night after night lift my praise to you your love is so good
You're my dream come true *(2xs)*

6 IN CHRIST

I WILL SING FOREVER OF YOUR LOVE

Chorus
I will sing forever of your love O Lord
I will sing forever of your love O Lord

I will sing forever of your love O Lord
Through all ages my mouth shall proclaim your truth
Of this I am sure that your love lasts for ever
That your truth is as firm as the heavens

Chorus
I will sing forever of your love O Lord
I will sing forever of your love O Lord

I have made a covenant with my chosen one
I have sworn to David my servant
I will establish your dynasty forever
And set up your throne through all ages

Chorus
I will sing forever of your love O Lord
I will sing forever of your love O Lord

My truth and my love shall be with him
By my name his might shall be exalted
He will say to me 'you are my Father
My God, the rock who saves me'

Chorus
I will sing forever of your love O Lord
I will sing forever of your love O Lord *(2xs)*

Bridge
I will sing I will sing
I will sing of your love

I will sing of your love forever
I will sing of your love forever *(2xs)*

I will sing I will sing
I will sing of your love
I will sing of your love forever

I will sing I will sing
I will sing yeh yeh yeh
I will sing of your love forever

I will sing of your love forever
I will sing of your love forever *(2xs)*

THE GOD-MAN

There is no god but the Man
No name besides His
There is no man but the Son
The Earth's filled with Him

Chorus
He is Jesus
The God who took on flesh
He is Jesus
The Man upon the throne
The one who became us
And made us what He is
Sons of God

There is no gift but the Lamb
Who took us in Him
There is no greater love than this
All men are in Christ

Chorus
He is Jesus
The Saviour of the World

He is Jesus
The Father's yes to all
The one who became us
And made us what He is
Sons of God

He is Jesus
The Light of the world
He is Jesus
The Father's yes to all
The one who became us
And made us what He is
Sons of God

And made us what He is
Sons of God *(4xs)*

EXODUS

Chorus
And the children of Israel went into
The midst of the sea upon dry ground
And the waters returned
And covered the chariots
The horsemen and the host of Pharaoh
That went into the sea after them
But the children of Israel
Walked upon dry ground
In the midst of the sea

It all began when the Lord
Made a promise to Abraham
And confirmed it to Jacob
That Israel would become his special people
And Joseph went before him
To prepare a place for his brethren
Though imprisoned he rose to be
The governor of Egypt

And Jacob moved to Egypt
Israel sojourned in the land of Ham
He grew mighty and multiplied
And became exceedingly fruitful

But there rose a new Pharaoh
Who knew not Joseph
Who thought to make an end of them
By casting their male-born into the river
A man of the house of Levi
Took to wife a daughter of Levi
Who bore a handsome male child
Hid him then inside a basket laid him
The daughter of Pharaoh came to bathe
She took the basket from the river
She raised Moses as one of Egypt's princes
Thus the Lord prepared the way for them

Chorus
And the children of Israel went into
The midst of the sea upon dry ground
And the waters returned
And covered the chariots
The horsemen and the host of Pharaoh
That went into the sea after them
But the children of Israel
Walked upon dry ground
In the midst of the sea

And it came to pass in those days
That the child Moses grew and became strong
He slew one of the Egyptians
Who smote a Hebrew one of his brethren
And Moses fled from Egypt
When Pharaoh knew this and sought to kill him
He dwelled in Midian with Jethro the priest
And married his daughter Zipporah
The cries of Israel came to the Lord
And he came down to free them from hard bondage

To realize his promise to Isaac
That his seed possess the land of Canaan

And the Lord in the burning bush
Sent Moses as their liberator
He gave Aaron as his prophet
To accomplish his design on Israel
And Moses went down to Egypt
With great power from the Lord Almighty
Commanded Pharaoh thus says the Lord
Pharaoh let my people go
But Pharaoh's heart was hardened
He would not let the Hebrews go
So God stretched out his hand against Egypt
His wonders were seen in the land of the Nile

Chorus
And the children of Israel went into
The midst of the sea upon dry ground
And the waters returned
And covered the chariots
The horsemen and the host of Pharaoh
That went into the sea after them
But the children of Israel
Walked upon dry ground
In the midst of the sea

On the night of the Passover
The Lord smote the first-born of Egypt
He brought out his people Israel
As a shepherd led them towards the Promised Land
Israel came out of Egypt
With great substance as the Lord had foretold
Joseph's bones were carried along
He had prophesied this would happen
But Pharaoh went after them
Grieved for letting the Hebrews go
His heart as his servants' were further hardened
For God to have his great victory

And the Angel of the Lord came down
And placed a pillar of cloud between them
This gave light to Israel
But complete darkness it was to the Egyptians
And Moses stretched out his hand
Over the sea as the Lord commanded
A strong eastern wind divided the sea
In the night watch it was made dry ground
And the children of Israel
Went into the sea upon dry ground
But Pharaoh's host was destroyed by the waters
It was then that Israel sang to the Lord

Chorus 2
I will sing to the Lord our God
For he has triumphed gloriously
He has thrown into the sea
Horsemen and chariots
The Lord is my strength and song
The Lord is his name forever
The Lord is my salvation
Who is like to you O Lord my God

Chorus
And the children of Israel went into
The midst of the sea upon dry ground
And the waters returned
And covered the chariots
The horsemen and the host of Pharaoh
That went into the sea after them
But the children of Israel
Walked upon dry ground
In the midst of the sea

ADORATION

Birds that fly high and fly low
Of all their shape colour and size

Fishes that swim in the deep
Of thousand species and their kind
Animals that walk on land
In all their different families
Small great large tall big
They're living everyday to give

Chorus
Adoration Adoration
Adoration Adoration
Adoration Adoration
Adoration Adoration

People going out each day
People that stay at their homes
Children playing in the fields
Children on the learning ground
Men women boys girls and kids
Of all the continents and the isles
Black yellow red blue white
In all the earth one voice will rise

Chorus
Adoration Adoration
Adoration Adoration
Adoration Adoration
Adoration Adoration

In everything we say and do
As we go out as we come in
As we live in the family
As we stay in our quiet place
While we sit stand run eat talk
We sleep and dream of marvellous things
This is your life that we live
So all our being with all our heart

Chorus
Adoration Adoration

Adoration Adoration
Adoration Adoration
Adoration Adoration

IL EST FIDÈLE

Il a promis la vie éternelle
A ceux qui croient en son Fils
Il a promis la guérison pour tous
Par les plaies de Jésus
Nous sommes appelés à le proclamer
Il est bon il est bon
Il a fait des merveilles pour toi et pour moi
Il est Dieu à jamais

Chorus
Chantons mon Dieu il est fidèle
Chaque jour il assure
Chantons Jésus il est fidèle
Il a promis il réalise
Adorons-le il est fidèle
Bénissons-le louons Jésus
Adorons-le il est fidèle
Magnifions-le le Fils de Dieu

Il a promis la délivrance du monde
Par le sang de Jésus
Il a promis le bonheur et la joie
La paix en Son Esprit
Nous sommes appelés à le proclamer
Il est si merveilleux
Il a fait de nous ses héritiers en son Fils
Il est Dieu à jamais

Chorus
Chantons mon Dieu il est fidèle
Chaque jour il assure
Chantons Jésus il est fidèle

Il a promis il réalise
Adorons-le il est fidèle
Bénissons-le louons Jésus
Adorons-le il est fidèle
Magnifions-le le Fils de Dieu

Alléluia il est fidèle
Le Roi des rois le seul Seigneur
Alléluia il est fidèle l'Agneau de Dieu
Sauveur du Monde
Alléluia il est fidèle
Le Roi des rois le seul Seigneur
Alléluia il est fidèle l'Agneau de Dieu
Sauveur du Monde

SON OF JESUS

Jesus Son of Man
Son of Mary
Son of Joseph Son of David
Son of Jesse Son of Judah
Son of Israel Son of Isaac
Son of Abraham Son of Noah
Son of Adam
Jesus Son of God *(2xs)*

THE LOVELIEST OF ALL

Chorus
The Loveliest of All
His name is the Great I AM
He walks and he talks and he loves forever
He is Lord Sovereign over all
He is mighty and awesome in worship
Here he comes with salvation in His wings
He runs he sings and he laughs
Lift up your heads O you gates

Even be lifted up you everlasting doors
For the king of glory shall come in
The Lord mighty to save us
The Loveliest of All

Lovely One you're the Loveliest of All
At Jordan you seduced me
You told me come and see where you dwelleth
And I abode with you
Lovely One as you taught by the waters
My heart began to beat faster
Your eyes met mine
At your sight I was speechless
Left all to follow you

Bridge
And I will sing your praises
Men will talk of your fame
You have exalted your name forever
O Lovely One

Chorus
The Loveliest of All
His name is the Great I AM
He walks and he talks and he loves forever
He is Lord Sovereign over all
He is mighty and awesome in worship
Here he comes with salvation in His wings
He runs he sings and he laughs
Lift up your heads O you gates
Even be lifted up you everlasting doors
For the king of glory shall come in
The Lord mighty to save us
The Loveliest of All

Lovely One we will bless you forever
You walked upon the waters
You called me and your love pierced my soul
I wondered who you are

Lovely One you are lovely forever
At Mount Tabor we saw your glory
Lifted up from the cross to the throne
You draw all men to you

Bridge
And I will sing your praises
Men will joy in your grace
You have won salvation by yourself forever
O Lovely One

Chorus
The Loveliest of All
His name is the Great I AM
He walks and he talks and he loves forever
He is Lord Sovereign over all
He is mighty and awesome in worship
Here he comes with salvation in His wings
He runs he sings and he laughs
Lift up your heads O you gates
Even be lifted up you everlasting doors
For the king of glory shall come in
The Lord mighty to save us
The Loveliest of All

Lift up your heads O you gates
Even be lifted up you everlasting doors
For the king of glory shall come in
The Lord mighty to save us
The Loveliest of All

7 CHRIST IN YOU

YOU ARE MY SON

Chorus
You are my Son
It is I who have begotten you this day
You are my Son
It is I who have begotten you this day

Ask of the nations I will give to you
The ends of the earth is your heritage
The Almighty has sworn and He will not change
You are my Son forever
According to my heart's desire

I have birthed my Son upon the Holy Hills
Before the creation you have always been
I will declare the decree of the Almighty
He said to me 'You are my Son
Today I have become your Father'

The Lord's revelation to my Master, sit on my right
Till I make your enemies your footstool
Rule in the midst of your foes with the sceptre of power
You are a priest forever like Melchizedek of old

Sacrifice and offering thou wouldest not
But a body you have prepared for me
And said I Lo, I come to do your will
In the volume of the book it is written of me

Chorus
You are my Son
It is I who have begotten you this day
You are my Son
It is I who have begotten you this day

GOD ALMIGHTY

Jesus you are God Almighty
Jesus you are God Almighty
Jesus you are God Almighty
Jesus you are God Almighty

Instruments (8xs)

Chorus
You told me that I
I live in you forever
You told me that I
I dance with you
Who live in me
You told me that you
You love me always
And now you tell me that I
Am yours and you are mine

Jesus you are God Almighty
Jesus you are God Almighty
Jesus you are God Almighty
Jesus you are God Almighty

Instruments (8xs)

Chorus
You told me that I
I live in you forever
You told me that I
I dance with you
Who live in me
You told me that you
You love me always
And now you tell me that I
Am yours and you are mine

Jesus you are God Almighty

Jesus you are God Almighty
Jesus you are God Almighty
Jesus you are God Almighty

JERUSALEM REJOICE

Lift up your heads behold he comes
Prepare adorn yourself
Your Redeemer is at hand
Comfort, comfort my people
Speak peace to Jerusalem
Tell her the time of captivity
Has come to an end
Watchman look who comes over there
Glorious shinning like the morning star
Make haste open you wide the gates
The Lord victorious has come to you
Sing for joy lift your voice
Jerusalem
He has come to save you

Chorus
Jerusalem, Jerusalem
Rejoice, rejoice Jerusalem
The Lord your God in the midst of you
Immanuel is his name
O rejoice, rejoice Jerusalem
He has come to save you
No more tears no more cry
Shall be found in you
For the Holy One of Israel
Has made his dwelling place in you

The heaven is my throne
The earth my footstool
Where is the house that you build to me
And the place of my rest
For Zion's sake I will not keep quiet

For Jerusalem's sake I will not rest
Till her righteousness goes forth as brightness
And her salvation as a burning lamp
I will gather her as a hen gathers her young ones
I will rejoice in Jerusalem
As I purge you from all your iniquities
And make you clean by the blood of the Lamb
You'll be my people I'll be your God
Jerusalem
I am the Holy One in the midst of you

Chorus
Jerusalem, Jerusalem
Rejoice, rejoice Jerusalem
The Lord your God in the midst of you
Immanuel is his name
O rejoice, rejoice Jerusalem
He has come to save you
No more tears no more cry
Shall be found in you
For the Holy One of Israel
Has made his dwelling place in you

O rejoice, rejoice Jerusalem
He has come to save you
No more tears no more cry
Shall be found in you
For the Holy One of Israel
Has made his dwelling place in you

MARY'S SONG

And here I am now
Standing in your presence
And I bow down worship you alone
The angels of heaven shouting out your holy name
I give glory and praise forever *(2xs)*

Chorus
The Lord is good at all times
Bless his name forever
He has done great things for me *(2xs)*

And here I am now
Standing in your presence
And I bow down worship you alone
The angels of heaven shouting out your holy name
I give glory and praise forever

Chorus
The Lord is good at all times
Bless his name forever
He has done great things for me *(2xs)*

Bridge
Ria praise Ria praise Ria glory *(8xs)*

Chorus
The Lord is good at all times
Bless his name forever
He has done great things for me *(4xs)*

Bridge
Ria praise Ria praise Ria glory *(8xs +)*

CHRIST + NOTHING = EVERYTHING

Christ + Nothing Christ + Nothing
Christ + Nothing = Everything
Christ + Nothing Christ + Nothing
Christ + Nothing = Everything

Instruments (2xs)

Christ + Nothing Christ + Nothing
Christ + Nothing = Everything

Christ + Nothing Christ + Nothing
Christ + Nothing = Everything

Chorus
Jesus Christ is Lord
And God raised him from the dead
Saviour of the World
Righteousness wisdom holiness redemption
Jesus Christ is Lord
Captain of our salvation
Resurrection Life
Author finisher of faith
He is everything

Instruments (2xs)

Christ + Nothing Christ + Nothing
Christ + Nothing = Everything
Christ + Nothing Christ + Nothing
Christ + Nothing = Everything

Chorus
Jesus Christ is Lord
And God raised him from the dead
Saviour of the World
Righteousness wisdom holiness redemption
Jesus Christ is Lord
Captain of our salvation
Resurrection Life
Author finisher of faith
He is everything

Pause (2xs)

Instruments (2xs)

Christ + Nothing Christ + Nothing
Christ + Nothing = Everything *(4xs)*

THE LORD IS THE SONG THAT I SING

The Lord is the song that I sing
He's the melody on my lips every day
From my childhood
Here I know that his love is true
The Lord is the song that I sing

The Lord is the song that I sing
He's the message that's in my ears every night
From my childhood
Here I know he is faithful and true
The Lord is the song that I sing

The Lord is the song that I sing
He's the lyrics that that I chant all the time
From my childhood
Here I know that his grace never fails
The Lord is the song that I sing

The Lord is the song that I sing
He's the melody that I dance in the night
From my childhood
Here I know that he's good toward me
The Lord is the song that I sing

From my childhood
Here I know that his love is true
The Lord is the song that I sing *(2xs)*

CHRIST IS RISEN OR MAMI'S SONG

Chorus
Hallelujah Hallelujah Hallelujah Hallelujah
Hallelujah Hallelujah Hallelujah Hallelujah

Christ is Risen He has triumphed
Over death and hell even the grave

Jesus who died upon the cross
Now is Alive Hallelujah

Chorus
Hallelujah Hallelujah Hallelujah Hallelujah
Hallelujah Hallelujah Hallelujah Hallelujah

Christ is Risen the tomb is empty
The Holy One of God has overcome
He tasted death for every man
Now is Alive Hallelujah

Chorus
Hallelujah Hallelujah Hallelujah Hallelujah
Hallelujah Hallelujah Hallelujah Hallelujah

Christ is Risen nevermore to die
Death no longer has rule over him
This is the day that the Lord has made
Let us Rejoice Hallelujah

Chorus
Hallelujah Hallelujah Hallelujah Hallelujah
Hallelujah Hallelujah Hallelujah Hallelujah

BIBLIOGRAPHY

1. THE HOLY BIBLE

2. MARGARET NEWMELI, *ANOTHER DIMENSION*

   The Ultimate Amalgam (2017)
   Worlds Collide family, Friendship (2018)
   Tales of Captain Nootra Childhood (2018), Perfection (2020)
   Brotherhood, Sonship (2019), Return to Innocence (2020).

3. DR. SHAWN SMITH

   As Righteous As God (2010), *Fathered by God, The New Man in Christ, Jesus Christ + Nothing = Everything* (2012), *Teachings, Gospel of Christ Ministries.*

4. ANDREW WOMMACK

   Spirit, Soul & Body (2008), *Grace, The Power of the Gospel* (2018), *Whose Righteousness* (1998) Andrew Wommack Ministries, 1 Innovation Way, Woodland Park, CO 80863 www.awmi.net

5. DUANE SHERIFF

   Our Union with Christ (2020), *Identity Theft* (2017) Victory Life Church www.pastorduane.com

6. DON MOEN

   Give Thanks (1986, 1999), *Rivers of Joy* (1995), *God is Good – Worship with Don Moen* (1998).

7. PAUL WILBUR *Shalom Jerusalem* (1995), *Jerusalem Arise* (1999), *Up to Zion* (1991).).

8. BOB FITTS

   He will Save You (1996), *Sacrifice/Take My Healing to the Nations* (1991), *Comfort My People* (1994), *A Taste of Heaven* (1995).

9. HILLSONG

   Hope (2003), *Touching Heaven Changing Earth* (1998), *For this Cause* (2000), *Saviour King* (2007). *The Power of Your Love* (1992).

10. *NARUTO*

   Masashi Kishimoto, Shueisha, *Weekly Shonen Jump* (1999-2014);

11. *AVATAR: THE LAST AIRBENDER*

Michael Dante DiMartino, Bryan Konietzko: *(Avatar: The Legend of Aang)* Nickelodeon (2005 - 2008).

Margaret Newmeli: https://amazon.com/author/margaretnewmeli

Twitter: Margaret Newmeli http://twitter.com/NewmeliMargaret
Cartoon World https://www.facebook.com/newmelimargaret
Youtube: https://www.youtube.com/user/newmar81
DC Marvel Song: https://youtu.be/MFfI8ZijbtE
One Man: https://www.youtube.com/watch?v=gkwvIJRJONE
New Meli: https://facebook.com/sioux.nootra.1/
Blogger: Another Dimension
https://margaretnewmeli.blogspot.com
Blogger: Margaret Newmeli https://newmeli.blogspot.com
Another Dimension: The Ultimate Amalgam:
https://www.amazon.com/dp/1490924019
Worlds Collide https://www.amazon.com/dp/1974280144
Worlds Collide II https://www.amazon.com/dp/1975697944
Une Autre Dimension l'Amalgame Ultime:
https://www.amazon.com/dp/1978104847
Author Page https://www.amazon.com/-/e/B076MWGMP8
Another Dimension
https://www.facebook.com/theultimateamalgam/
Goodreads https://www.goodreads.com/margaretnewmeli
All Author newmar.allauthor.com

ABOUT THE AUTHOR

Margaret Newmeli sings the *Saviour of the World*. She's the author of *Another Dimension: The Ultimate Amalgam, Worlds Collide, Tales of Captain Nootra, Perfection*. The Lord is the Song that I sing.
"And we have seen and do testify that the Father sent the Son to be the Saviour of the world." *1Jn. 4:14.* "God our Saviour will have all men to be saved, and to come unto the knowledge of the truth." *1Tim. 2:3,4.*

I have put my trust in the love of God toward me.